Bengal Tigers

By Christy Steele

Steadwell Books

Raintree Steck-Vaughn Publishers

A Harcourt Company

Austin · New York

www.raintreesteckvaughn.com

ANIMALS OF THE RAIN FOREST

Published by Raintree Steck-Vaughn Publishers, an imprint of Steck-Vaughn Company.

Library of Congress Cataloging-in-Publication Data
ISBN 0-7398-5369-4
Printed and bound in the United States of America
1 2 3 4 5 6 7 8 9 10 WZ 05 04 03 02

Produced by Compass Books

Photo Acknowledgments
Digital Stock, cover, 16; Root Resources/Kenneth Fink, title page, 28–29; Visuals Unlimited/Kjell Sandved, 6; Matt Tierney Jr., 8; Joe McDonald, 11, 18; Mark Newman, 12; Tom Walker, 15, 26; Robert Barber, 21; Guillermo Gonzalez, 22; Mindy Hackett, 24.

Editor: Bryon Cahill
Consultant: Sean Dolan

Content Consultant
Ron Tilson
Tiger Information Center

This book supports the National Science Standards.

Contents

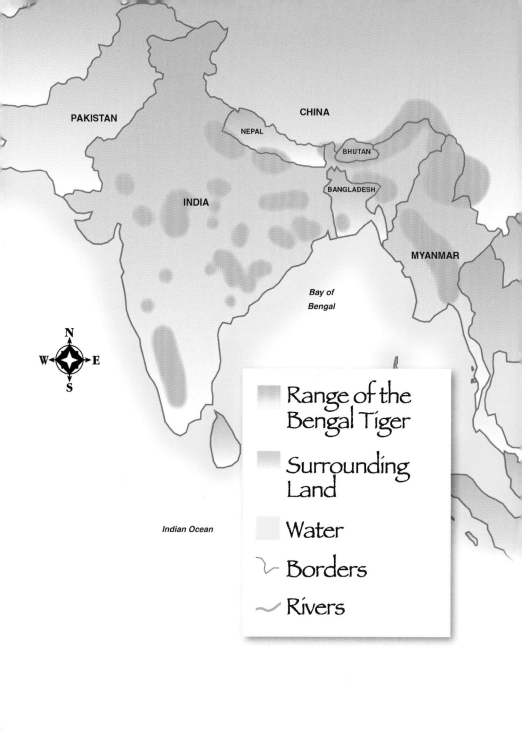

PAKISTAN

CHINA

NEPAL

BHUTAN

BANGLADESH

INDIA

MYANMAR

Bay of
Bengal

N
W E
S

Range of the
Bengal Tiger

Surrounding
Land

Water

Borders

Rivers

Indian Ocean

4

A Quick Look at Bengal Tigers

What do Bengal tigers look like?

Most Bengal tigers have orange fur with black stripes and white stomachs. Some Bengal tigers are white with black stripes.

Where do Bengal tigers live?

Bengal tigers live in the rain forests and mangrove swamps of India.

What do Bengal tigers eat?

Bengal tigers eat only meat. Common foods are deer, wild pigs, and monkeys. They sometimes hunt porcupines.

You can see the round black pupils in this Bengal tiger's eyes.

Bengal Tigers in the Rain Forest

Bengal tigers are one of five kinds of tigers. All tigers are big cats. Big cats have round **pupils** in their eyes instead of slits, like small housecats do. A pupil is the black opening in the eye through which light passes. Big cats can also roar. Other big cats include lions, leopards, and jaguars. Tigers are the most powerful of all the big cats.

The scientific name for Bengal tigers is *Panthera tigris*. Panthera means big cat. Tigris is from a Greek word that means stripes. Like all tigers, Bengal tigers have black stripes on their coat.

Bengal tigers are named after Bengal, India, where many of them live. They make their homes in the thick rain forests there. Rain forests are places where many trees and plants grow close together and much rain falls.

▲ Bengal tigers swim more than any other kind of big cat.

Where Do Bengal Tigers Live?

Bengal tigers live in the rain forests of India. Many also live in the mangrove swamps of Bangladesh and Bengal. In these areas, mangrove trees grow in wet, soggy ground.

Bengal tigers are suited to live in rain forest **habitats**. A habitat is a place where an animal or plant usually lives. The trees provide places for Bengal tigers to hide as they hunt for food.

Bengal tigers have their own territories. A territory is land that an animal lives on and fights to keep for itself. Bengal tigers usually live alone in their territories. They need up to 80 square miles (207 sq km) to hunt for food. A male's territory is usually larger than a female's territory. At times, female tigers may even live in small parts of a male's territory.

When they find a territory, Bengal tigers mark it with special scents. Sometimes they also scratch trees. These things warn other tigers to stay away. The scents also tell other tigers important information about the size and **gender** of the tiger that lives in the territory.

Bengal tigers make several dens throughout their territories. A den is a small place where an animal lives. The dens may be in caves, thick grass, or bushes. When they are tired, the Bengal tigers sleep in whatever den is closest to them.

Water, such as a stream or river, is often part of a Bengal tiger's territory. They are excellent swimmers and will hunt in water. They usually swim to cool down during hot weather.

What Do Bengal Tigers Look Like?

Bengal tigers are medium-sized tigers with long, muscular bodies. Males grow to about 9.5 feet (2.9 m) long. Females grow up to 8 feet (2.4 m) long. Males usually weigh about 480 pounds (218 kg), and females weigh about 300 pounds (136 kg).

Like all tigers, Bengals have round heads and ears. They have muscular shoulders and narrow hips. They have short, strong legs and can jump up to 16 feet (5 m). Their tails are up to 4 feet (1.2 m) long, and they use them to balance themselves when they jump or climb trees.

Most Bengal tigers have short orange fur with many black stripes. White fur covers their stomach. Tigers with this coloring have yellow eyes. A few Bengal tigers are white with black stripes. White tigers have blue eyes.

Tiger stripes are unique, or one of a kind, like human fingerprints. Each tiger has its own stripe pattern. Even the two sides of a tiger are marked differently.

Like all tigers, Bengal tigers have five toes on their front paws and four toes on their back paws. A tiger's paw prints are called pug marks.

Each tiger's stripes are unique. No other tiger has stripes just like this one's.

The pug, or foot pad, is the soft covering that protects a tiger's foot.

Bengal tigers have sharp claws that grow up to 5 inches (13 cm) long. Like all cats, their claws are **retractable**. Retractable means that something can be pulled in or back. Bengal tigers pull their claws inside their paws to walk or run quietly. They push their claws out to hunt, dig, scratch, or climb trees.

This Bengal tiger is eating meat from prey that it has caught.

What Bengal Tigers Eat

Bengal tigers are **carnivores**. A carnivore is an animal that eats only meat. A Bengal needs about 13 pounds (6 kg) of meat each day to live.

Bengal tigers are predators. Predators hunt other animals for food. Prey are animals that are hunted and eaten. Bengal tigers usually hunt large animals because they contain more meat than smaller animals. Deer, water buffalo, wild pigs, and monkeys are common prey of Bengal tigers.

Bengals can get hurt when they hunt. Wild pigs have sharp horns that can stab and kill them. Porcupines sometimes shoot their quills at Bengal tigers. Quills are like long needles. Quills stuck in a paw or jaw can be very painful. If it is hurt, a tiger cannot hunt well. It may starve to death if it cannot hunt enough food.

Hunting

Most Bengal tigers are **nocturnal**. This means they are active at night. Their sharp senses help them hunt for food. Bengals see six times better at night than people do. But while hunting, hearing is the Bengal's most important sense. Bengal tigers can hear up to five times better than people do. They find prey by listening for the sound of animals moving through the rain forest.

It is easier for Bengal tigers to hunt at night because they are harder to see then. Their stripes provide **camouflage** in the rain forest. Camouflage is coloring or patterns that help an animal blend in with its natural surroundings. A tiger's uneven stripes help make its body blend in with trees, grasses, or bushes.

Bengal tigers hunt by sneaking up on their prey and pouncing on it. Pouncing is a sudden attack. Most other big cats hunt by running after prey. Running after prey does not work well for Bengal tigers. They can run up to 35 miles (56 km) per hour for short periods, but lose speed running over long distances. Prey may get away if the Bengal has to chase it too far.

This tiger is walking along an animal trail to find prey.

Bengal tigers usually walk along animal trails, stream beds, and beside water holes to find prey. If they see prey, they quietly follow it. This is called stalking. Bengal tigers hide in trees or tall grasses until they can sneak up and attack their prey from behind. Bengal tigers sometimes hide and wait for an animal to approach them. Once their prey comes near, they pounce on it.

You can see this Bengal tiger's sharp canine teeth.

Eating

Bengal tigers usually try to find old, sick, or young prey. These animals are slower and easier to catch. Bengals jump on their prey and use their long, sharp claws to grab them. Their strong jaws and 30 sharp teeth help them kill and hold prey.

Bengal tigers break the spine of small or medium-sized prey by biting their necks. Bengals bite with two long canine teeth that are the size of a man's middle finger. With a broken spine, prey is unable to move. If a prey animal is larger, Bengals will attack by biting the throat. The throat bite makes the animal unable to breathe and kills it.

After the prey dies, Bengal tigers drag the body to a safe hiding place. They may cover the prey with leaves or branches. Over several days, the Bengal tigers return to eat everything, except the prey's stomach and bones. A Bengal tiger can eat up to 66 pounds (30 kg) of meat at a time.

Bengal tigers slice meat from prey with their canine teeth. They use their short incisor teeth to help tear meat from bones. Other teeth help the tiger chew and grind meat. Their rough tongues and throats are covered by hundreds of hook-like bumps called papillae. Papillae help Bengal tigers scrape meat off the prey's bones.

After eating a large animal, Bengal tigers are usually not hungry for several days. They sleep and rest until their next hunt. They usually have to go hunting about 10 times before they catch any prey.

Tigers usually come together only during the mating season.

A Bengal Tiger's Life Cycle

Most Bengal tigers begin mating when they are about four years old. Their mating season is in the spring. To find mates, males and females often roar. They may also spray special scents around their territories. This lets other tigers know that they are ready to mate. When mating, males and females spend about one week with each other. Then, they return to their territories alone.

After mating, females search for a den where they can give birth. They look for a den in a hidden place. Enemies, such as male tigers and other large animals, may try to catch newborn Bengal tigers. If the den is hidden, the newborn tigers will be safer.

Cubs

About 15 weeks after mating, females give birth to two to four newborn tigers, called cubs. For the first six to eight weeks, cubs drink only milk from their mothers' bodies.

After about six weeks, females start bringing meat back to their cubs. Females need to hunt to find this food. They leave their cubs alone in the den while they search for prey. Cubs are in danger during this time. Many cubs are caught by predators and do not live to become adults.

Cubs learn skills by hunting with their mothers. Cubs practice these hunting skills by playing. They stalk, pounce, and chase each other. By the time they are 18 months old, cubs are able to hunt by themselves.

Cubs usually live with their mothers until they are one to three years old. A group of tigers that lives together is called a streak or an ambush. Once they are old enough, the cubs leave to find their own territories.

Bengal tigers in the wild live 10 to 15 years. In zoos, they may live up to 26 years.

These Bengal tiger cubs are playing with each other.

This Bengal tiger is sitting in a water hole to cool off.

A Day in the Life of a Bengal Tiger

Most Bengal tigers rest in dens during the hottest parts of the day. They also swim or splash in water holes to cool off.

Bengal tigers spend most of their time alone. They patrol, or walk around, their territories to make sure other tigers are not around. Bengal tigers will fight any other tigers that enter their territory. They also make signposts. Signposts are things such as scents or claw marks that mark the edges of their territories.

Most Bengal tigers' nights are spent hunting. They use their whiskers to help them move quietly through the rain forest. These long whiskers are on their head, body, and the back of their front legs. The whiskers sense changes in the air as the Bengals move close to objects. This information helps the tigers move around objects instead of bumping into them. It also helps the Bengals sense how small a space is. If the whiskers can fit through a space, the tigers know that the rest of their body can, too.

Bengal tigers are clean animals. They spend part of their day **grooming**, or cleaning, themselves. They do this by licking their bodies with their rough tongues. They also lick their paws and rub them across their ears and head. Tigers also groom each other. Mothers groom their cubs. Males and females groom each other during mating season. Bengals will also lick any wounds they have. The tongue covers the wound with special saliva that cleans it and helps it heal. Saliva is a watery mixture made in the mouth.

This Bengal tiger is sleeping peacefully.

The Future of Bengal Tigers

There were once eight kinds of tigers. Today, there are only five left—the Bengal, Siberian, Sumatran, Indochinese, and Caspian. The Bengal tiger is the most common kind of tiger. But it is still in danger of becoming **extinct**. Extinct means that there are no more of that **species** of animal living. Scientists think there are only from 3,000 to 5,000 Bengal tigers left in the wild.

The main reason that Bengal tigers are in danger is because the rain forest is disappearing. People cut down the forests to build houses, towns, and roads. Without the rain forest, Bengal tigers do not have enough land for territories. Without large territories in which to hunt, they cannot find enough food to eat. Tigers, like most animals, die without food.

This tiger lives in a reserve. It is against the law to hunt tigers there.

Poaching

Bengal tigers are also in danger because people hunt them. Hunters use the skins to make rugs and coats. Other people believe a tiger's body parts have healing powers. People sell these body parts as medicine.

 Bengal tigers have white spots on the backs of their ears. Scientists think the spots might help tigers see each other at night. Or a tiger may turn its ears so the spots show at the front. This warns other tigers to stay away.

Some people are trying to save Bengal tigers. They are working with governments to make laws to protect tigers. In many countries, it is against the law to kill tigers or to buy and sell their body parts. Still, people hunt Bengal tigers. Hunting animals when it is against the law is called **poaching**. Poaching limits the number of Bengal tigers in the wild.

What Will Happen to Bengal Tigers?

Most Bengal tigers live in India. In 1972, the Indian government and the World Wide Fund for Nature started Project Tiger. This project works to keep tigers safe.

Today, there are more than 40 tiger reserves throughout India. A reserve is a place where guards make sure poachers cannot kill tigers. If people keep working together, Bengal tigers will survive for a long time to come.

stripes
see page 7

tail
see page 10

legs
see page 10

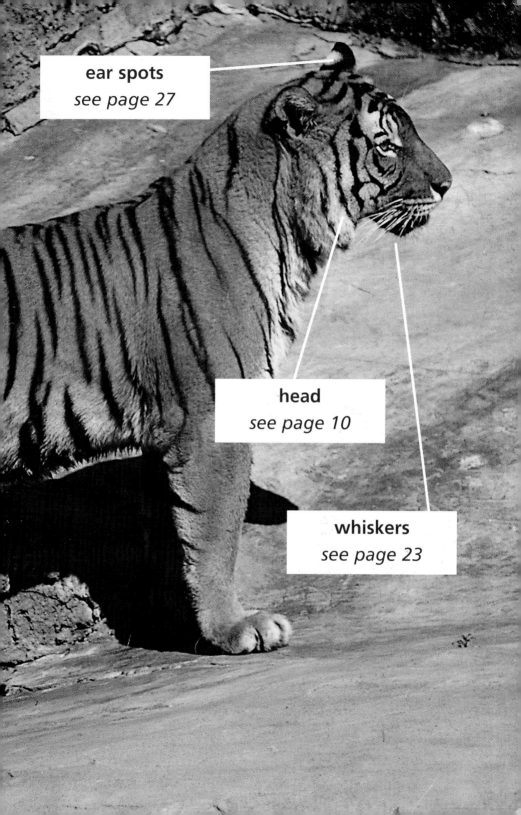

ear spots
see page 27

head
see page 10

whiskers
see page 23

Glossary

camouflage (KAM-uh-flahj)—colors, shapes, and patterns that help an animal blend in with its background

carnivores (KAHR-nuh-vors)—animals that eat only meat

extinct (ek-STINKT)—when all of one kind of animal has died out

gender (JEN-dur)—whether a person or creature is male or female

grooming (GROO-ming)—to clean itself or other animals

habitats (HAB-i-tats)—places where an animal or plant usually lives

nocturnal (nok-TUR-nuhl)—active at night

poaching (POH-ching)—to catch fish or kill animals when it is against the law

pupils (PYOO-puhls)—the black openings in the eyes through which light passes

retractable (re-TRAKT-uh-buhl)—the ability to pull in and push out

species (SPEE-sees)—a group of animals or plants most closely related to each other

Internet Sites

Tiger Information Center
www.5tigers.org

Tiger Territory
www.lairweb.org.nz/tiger

Useful Address

Tiger Information Center
13000 Zoo Boulevard
Apple Valley, MN 55124

Books to Read

Middleton, Don. *Tigers.* New York: PowerKids
Press, 1999.

Welsbacher, Anne. *Tigers.* Edina, MN: Abdo &
Daughters, 2000.

Index